DEC. 2010

Test Results for Mobile Device Acquisition Tool:
iXAM Version 1.5.6

NCJ 232384

John H. Laub
Director, National Institute of Justice

This report was prepared for the National Institute of Justice, U.S. Department of Justice, by the Office of Law Enforcement Standards of the National Institute of Standards and Technology under Interagency Agreement 2003–IJ–R–029.

The National Institute of Justice is a component of the Office of Justice Programs, which also includes the Bureau of Justice Assistance, the Bureau of Justice Statistics, the Office of Juvenile Justice and Delinquency Prevention, and the Office for Victims of Crime.

December 2010

Test Results for Mobile Device Acquisition Tool:
iXAM Version 1.5.6

**National Institute of
Standards and Technology**
U.S. Department of Commerce

Introduction

The Computer Forensics Tool Testing (CFTT) program is a joint project of the National Institute of Justice (NIJ), the department of Homeland Security (DHS), and the National Institute of Standards and Technology Office of Law Enforcement Standards (OLES) and Information Technology Laboratory (ITL). CFTT is supported by other organizations, including the Federal Bureau of Investigation, the U.S. Department of Defense Cyber Crime Center, U.S. Internal Revenue Service Criminal Investigation Division Electronic Crimes Program, and the U.S. Department of Homeland Security's Bureau of Immigration and Customs Enforcement, U.S. Customs and Border Protection and U.S. Secret Service. The objective of the CFTT program is to provide measurable assurance to practitioners, researchers, and other applicable users that the tools used in computer forensics investigations provide accurate results. Accomplishing this requires the development of specifications and test methods for computer forensics tools and subsequent testing of specific tools against those specifications.

Test results provide the information necessary for developers to improve tools, users to make informed choices, and the legal community and others to understand the tools' capabilities. This approach to testing computer forensic tools is based on well–recognized methodologies for conformance and quality testing. The specifications and test methods posted on the CFTT Web site (http://www.cftt.nist.gov/) are available for review and comment by the computer forensics community.

This document reports the results from testing iXAM, version 1.5.6, against the *Smart Phone Tool Test Assertions and Test Plan*, available at the CFTT Web site (www.cftt.nist.gov/mobile_devices.htm).

Test results from other software packages and the CFTT tool methodology can be found on NIJ's computer forensics tool testing Web

page, http://www.ojp.usdoj.gov/nij/topics/technology/electronic–crime/cftt.htm.

How to Read This Report

This report is divided into five sections. The first section is a summary of the results from the test runs. This section is sufficient for most readers to assess the suitability of the tool for the intended use. The remaining sections of the report describe how the tests were conducted and provide documentation of test case run details that support the report summary. Sections 2 and 3 provide justification for the selection of test cases and assertions from the set of possible cases defined in the test plan for smart phone forensic tools. The test cases are selected, in general, based on features offered by the tool. Section 4 lists the hardware and software used to run the test cases. Section 5 contains a description of each test case, test assertions used in the test case, the expected result and the actual result.

Test Results for Mobile Device Data Acquisition Tool

Tool Tested:	iXAM
Version:	1.5.6
Run Environment:	Windows XP Service Pack 2
Supplier:	Forensic Telecommunications Services
Address:	PO Box 242, Sevenoaks TN15 6ZT
Tel:	+44 (0)1732 459811
Fax:	+44 (0)1732 741261
WWW:	http://www.forensicts.co.uk

1 Results Summary

The tested tool acquired all supported data objects completely and accurately from the selected test mobile device (i.e., iPhone 3G). No anomalies were found.

2 Test Case Selection

Test cases used to test mobile device acquisition tools are defined in *Smart Phone Tool Test Assertions and Test Plan Version 1.0*. To test a tool, test cases are selected from the *Test Plan* document based on the features offered by the tool. Not all test cases or test assertions are appropriate for all tools. There is a core set of base cases that are executed for every tool tested. Tool features guide the selection of additional test cases. If a given tool implements a given feature then the test cases linked to that feature are run. Table 1a lists the test cases available in iXAM. Table 2a lists the test cases not available in iXAM.

Table 1a: Selected Test Cases (iPhone 3G)

Supported Test Cases	Cases Selected for Execution
Base Cases	SPT–01, SPT–02, SPT–03, SPT–04, SPT–05, SPT–06, SPT–07, SPT–08, SPT–09, SPT–10, SPT–11, SPT–12, SPT–13
Acquire SIM memory over supported interfaces (e.g., PC/SC reader).	SPT–14
Attempt acquisition of a non–supported SIM.	SPT–15
Begin SIM acquisition and interrupt connectivity by interface disengagement.	SPT–16
Acquire SIM memory and review reported subscriber and equipment related information (i.e., SPN, ICCID, IMSI, MSISDN).	SPT–17
Acquire SIM memory and review reported Abbreviated	SPT–18

Supported Test Cases	Cases Selected for Execution
Dialing Numbers (ADN).	
Acquire SIM memory and review reported Last Numbers Dialed (LND).	SPT–19
Acquire SIM memory and review reported text messages (SMS, EMS).	SPT–20
Acquire SIM memory and review recoverable deleted text messages (SMS, EMS).	SPT–21
Acquire SIM memory and review reported location related data (i.e., LOCI, GPRSLOCI).	SPT–22
Acquire SIM memory by selecting a combination of supported data elements.	SPT–23
Acquire mobile device internal memory and review reported data via supported generated report formats.	SPT–24
Acquire SIM memory and review reported data via supported generated report formats.	SPT–26
Attempt acquisition of a password–protected SIM.	SPT–28
Perform a physical acquisition and review data output for readability.	SPT–31
Perform a physical acquisition and review reports for recoverable deleted data.	SPT–32
Acquire mobile device internal memory and review data containing non–ASCII characters.	SPT–33
Acquire SIM memory and review data containing non–ASCII characters.	SPT–34
Begin acquisition on a PIN protected SIM to determine if the tool provides an accurate count of the remaining number of PIN attempts and if the PIN attempts are decremented when entering an incorrect value.	SPT–35
Begin acquisition on a SIM whose PIN attempts have been exhausted to determine if the tool provides an accurate count of the remaining number of PUK attempts and if the PUK attempts are decremented when entering an incorrect value.	SPT–36
Acquire mobile device internal memory and review hash values for vendor supported data objects.	SPT–38
Acquire SIM memory and review hash values for vendor supported data objects.	SPT–39

Table 2a: Omitted Test Cases (iPhone 3G)

Unsupported Test Cases	Cases omitted – not executed
Acquire mobile device internal memory and review reported data via the preview pane.	SPT–25
Acquire SIM memory and review reported data via the preview–pane.	SPT–27

Unsupported Test Cases	Cases omitted – not executed
After a successful mobile device internal memory, alter the case file via third–party means and attempt to re–open the case.	SPT–29
After a successful SIM acquisition, alter the case file via third–party means and attempt to re–open the case.	SPT–30
Perform a stand–alone mobile device internal memory acquisition and review the status flags for text messages present on the SIM.	SPT–37
Acquire mobile device internal memory and review data containing GPS longitude and latitude coordinates.	SPT–40

3 Results by Test Assertion

Table 3a summarizes the test results by assertion. The column labeled **Assertion** gives the text of each assertion. The column labeled **Tests** gives the number of test cases that use the given assertion. The column labeled **Anomaly** gives the section number in this report where the anomaly is discussed.

Table 3a: Assertions Tested: (iPhone 3G)

Assertions Tested	Tests	Anomaly
SPT–CA–01 If a cellular forensic tool provides support for connectivity of the target device then the tool shall successfully recognize the target device via all vendor supported interfaces (e.g., cable, Bluetooth, IrDA).	1	
SPT–CA–02 If a cellular forensic tool attempts to connect to a non–supported device then the tool shall notify the user that the device is not supported.	1	
SPT–CA–03 If connectivity between the mobile device and cellular forensic tool is disrupted then the tool shall notify the user that connectivity has been disrupted.	1	
SPT–CA–04 If a cellular forensic tool completes acquisition of the target device without error then the tool shall have the ability to present acquired data objects in a useable format via either a preview–pane or generated report.	2	
SPT–CA–05 If a cellular forensic tool completes acquisition of the target device without error then subscriber–related information shall be presented in a useable format.	1	
SPT–CA–06 If a cellular forensic tool completes acquisition of the target device without error then equipment related information shall be presented in a useable format.	1	
SPT–CA–07 If a cellular forensic tool completes acquisition of the target device without error then address book entries shall be presented in a useable format.	1	
SPT–CA–08 If a cellular forensic tool completes acquisition of the target device without error then maximum length address book entries shall be presented in a useable format.	1	

Assertions Tested	Tests	Anomaly
SPT–CA–09 If a cellular forensic tool completes acquisition of the target device without error then address book entries containing special characters shall be presented in a useable format.	1	
SPT–CA–10 If a cellular forensic tool completes acquisition of the target device without error then address book entries containing blank names shall be presented in a useable format.	1	
SPT–CA–11 If a cellular forensic tool completes acquisition of the target device without error then email addresses associated with address book entries shall be presented in a useable format.	1	
SPT–CA–12 If a cellular forensic tool completes acquisition of the target device without error then graphics associated with address book entries shall be presented in a useable format.	1	
SPT–CA–13 If a cellular forensic tool completes acquisition of the target device without error then datebook, calendar, note entries shall be presented in a useable format.	1	
SPT–CA–14 If a cellular forensic tool completes acquisition of the target device without error then maximum length datebook, calendar, note entries shall be presented in a useable format.	1	
SPT–CA–15 If a cellular forensic tool completes acquisition of the target device without error then call logs (incoming/outgoing/missed) shall be presented in a useable format.	1	
SPT–CA–16 If a cellular forensic tool completes acquisition of the target device without error then the corresponding date/time stamps and the duration of the call for call logs shall be presented in a useable format.	1	
SPT–CA–17 If a cellular forensic tool completes acquisition of the target device without error then ASCII text messages (i.e., SMS, EMS) shall be presented in a useable format.	1	
SPT–CA–18 If a cellular forensic tool completes acquisition of the target device without error then the corresponding date/time stamps for text messages shall be presented in a useable format.	1	
SPT–CA–19 If a cellular forensic tool completes acquisition of the target device without error then the corresponding status (i.e., read, unread) for text messages shall be presented in a useable format.	1	
SPT–CA–20 If a cellular forensic tool completes acquisition of the target device without error then the corresponding sender / recipient phone numbers for text messages shall be presented in a useable format.	1	
SPT–CA–21 If a cellular forensic tool completes acquisition of the target device without error then MMS messages and associated audio shall be presented in a useable format.	1	
SPT–CA–22 If a cellular forensic tool completes acquisition of the target device without error then MMS messages and associated graphic files shall be presented in a useable format.	1	
SPT–CA–23 If a cellular forensic tool completes acquisition of the target device without error then MMS messages and associated video	1	

Assertions Tested	Tests	Anomaly
shall be presented in a useable format.		
SPT–CA–24 If a cellular forensic tool completes acquisition of the target device without error then stand–alone audio files shall be presented in a useable format via either an internal application or suggested third–party application.	1	
SPT–CA–25 If a cellular forensic tool completes acquisition of the target device without error then stand–alone graphic files shall be presented in a useable format via either an internal application or suggested third–party application.	1	
SPT–CA–26 If a cellular forensic tool completes acquisition of the target device without error then stand–alone video files shall be presented in a useable format via either an internal application or suggested third–party application.	1	
SPT–CA–27 If a cellular forensic tool completes acquisition of the target device without error then device specific application related data shall be acquired and presented in a useable format via either an internal application or suggested third–party application.	1	
SPT–CA–28 If a cellular forensic tool completes acquisition of the target device without error then Internet related data (i.e., bookmarks, visited sites) cached to the device shall be acquired and presented in a useable format.	1	
SPT–CA–30 If a cellular forensic tool provides the user with a "Select All" individual device data objects then the tool shall complete the acquisition of all individually selected data objects without error.	2	
SPT–CA–32 If a cellular forensic tool completes two consecutive logical acquisitions of the target device without error then the payload (data objects) on the mobile device shall remain consistent.	1	
SPT–AO–01 If a cellular forensic tool provides support for connectivity of the target SIM then the tool shall successfully recognize the target SIM via all tool–supported interfaces (e.g., PC/SC reader, proprietary reader, smart phone itself).	2	
SPT–AO–02 If a cellular forensic tool attempts to connect to a non–supported SIM then the tool shall notify the user that the SIM is not supported.	1	
SPT–AO–03 If a cellular forensic tool loses connectivity with the SIM reader then the tool shall notify the user that connectivity has been disrupted.	1	
SPT–AO–04 If a cellular forensic tool completes acquisition of the target SIM without error then the SPN shall be presented in a useable format.	1	
SPT–AO–05 If a cellular forensic tool completes acquisition of the target SIM without error then the ICCID shall be presented in a useable format.	1	
SPT–AO–06 If a cellular forensic tool completes acquisition of the target SIM without error then the IMSI shall be presented in a useable	1	

Assertions Tested	Tests	Anomaly
format.		
SPT–AO–07 If a cellular forensic tool completes acquisition of the target SIM without error then the MSISDN shall be presented in a useable format.	1	
SPT–AO–08 If a cellular forensic tool completes acquisition of the target SIM without error then ASCII Abbreviated Dialing Numbers (ADN) shall be presented in a useable format.	1	
SPT–AO–09 If a cellular forensic tool completes acquisition of the target SIM without error then maximum length ADNs shall be presented in a useable format.	1	
SPT–AO–10 If a cellular forensic tool completes acquisition of the SIM without error then ADNs containing special characters shall be presented in a useable format.	1	
SPT–AO–11 If a cellular forensic tool completes acquisition of the SIM without error then ADNs containing blank names shall be presented in a useable format.	1	
SPT–AO–12 If a cellular forensic tool completes acquisition of the target SIM without error then Last Numbers Dialed (LND) shall be presented in a useable format.	1	
SPT–AO–13 If a cellular forensic tool completes acquisition of the target SIM without error then the corresponding date/time stamps for LNDs shall be presented in a useable format.	1	
SPT–AO–14 If a cellular forensic tool completes acquisition of the target SIM without error then ASCII SMS text messages shall be presented in a useable format.	1	
SPT–AO–15 If a cellular forensic tool completes acquisition of the target SIM without error then ASCII EMS text messages shall be presented in a useable format.	1	
SPT–AO–16 If a cellular forensic tool completes acquisition of the target SIM without error then the corresponding date/time stamps for all text messages shall be presented in a useable format.	1	
SPT–AO–17 If a cellular forensic tool completes acquisition of the target SIM without error then the corresponding status (i.e., read, unread) for text messages shall be presented in a useable format.	1	
SPT–AO–18 If a cellular forensic tool completes acquisition of the target SIM without error then the corresponding sender / recipient phone numbers for text messages shall be presented in a useable format.	1	
SPT–AO–19 If the cellular forensic tool completes acquisition of the target SIM without error then deleted text messages that have not been overwritten shall be presented in a useable format.	1	
SPT–AO–20 If a cellular forensic tool completes acquisition of the target SIM without error then location related data (i.e., LOCI) shall be presented in a useable format.	1	
SPT–AO–21 If a cellular forensic tool completes acquisition of the target SIM without error then location related data (i.e., GRPSLOCI)	1	

Assertions Tested	Tests	Anomaly
shall be presented in a useable format.		
SPT–AO–23 If a cellular forensic tool provides the user with an "Select All" individual SIM data objects then the tool shall complete the acquisition of all individually selected data objects without error.	1	
SPT–AO–25 If a cellular forensic tool completes acquisition of the SIM without error then the tool shall present the acquired data in a useable format via supported generated report formats.	2	
SPT–AO–28 If the SIM is password–protected then the cellular forensic tool shall provide the examiner with the opportunity to input the PIN before acquisition.	1	
SPT–AO–29 If a cellular forensic tool provides the examiner with the remaining number of authentication attempts then the application should provide an accurate count of the remaining PIN attempts.	1	
SPT–AO–30 If a cellular forensic tool provides the examiner with the remaining number of PUK attempts then the application should provide an accurate count of the remaining PUK attempts.	1	
SPT–AO–31 If the cellular forensic tool supports a physical acquisition of the target device then the tool shall complete the acquisition without error.	1	
SPT–AO–32 If the cellular forensic tool supports the interpretation of address book entries present on the target device then the tool shall report recoverable active and deleted data or address book data remnants in a useable format.	1	
SPT–AO–33 If the cellular forensic tool supports the interpretation of calendar, tasks, or notes present on the target device then the tool shall report recoverable active and deleted calendar, tasks, or note data remnants in a useable format.	1	
SPT–AO–34 If the cellular forensic tool supports the interpretation of call logs present on the target device then the tool shall report recoverable active and deleted call or call log data remnants in a useable format.	1	
SPT–AO–35 If the cellular forensic tool supports the interpretation of SMS messages present on the target device then the tool shall report recoverable active and deleted SMS messages or SMS message data remnants in a useable format.	1	
SPT–AO–36 If the cellular forensic tool supports the interpretation of EMS messages present on the target device then the tool shall report recoverable active and deleted EMS messages or EMS message data remnants in a useable format.	1	
SPT–AO–37 If the cellular forensic tool supports the interpretation of audio files present on the target device then the tool shall report recoverable active and deleted audio data or audio file data remnants in a useable format.	1	
SPT–AO–38 If the cellular forensic tool supports the interpretation of graphic files present on the target device then the tool shall report	1	

Assertions Tested	Tests	Anomaly
recoverable active and deleted graphic file data or graphic file data remnants in a useable format.		
SPT–AO–39 If the cellular forensic tool supports the interpretation of video files present on the target device then the tool shall report recoverable active and deleted video file data or video file data remnants in a useable format.	1	
SPT–AO–40 If the cellular forensic tool supports display of non–ASCII characters then the application should present ADNs in their native format.	2	
SPT–AO–41 If the cellular forensic tool supports proper display of non–ASCII characters then the application should present text messages in their native format.	2	
SPT–AO–43 If the cellular forensic tool supports hashing for individual data objects then the tool shall present the user with a hash value for each supported data object.	2	

Table 4a lists the assertions that were not tested, usually due to the tool not supporting an optional feature.

Table 4a: Assertions Not Tested (iPhone 3G)

Assertions Not Tested
SPT–CA–29 If a cellular forensic tool provides the user with an "Acquire All" device data objects acquisition option then the tool shall complete the acquisition of all data objects without error.
SPT–CA–31 If a cellular forensic tool provides the user with the ability to "Select Individual" device data objects for acquisition then the tool shall acquire each exclusive data object without error.
SPT–AO–22 If a cellular forensic tool provides the user with an "Acquire All" SIM data objects acquisition option then the tool shall complete the acquisition of all data objects without error.
SPT–AO–24 If a cellular forensic tool provides the user with the ability to "Select Individual" SIM data objects for acquisition then the tool shall acquire each exclusive data object without error.
SPT–AO–26 If a cellular forensic tool completes acquisition of the target device / SIM without error then the tool shall present the acquired data in a useable format in a preview–pane view.
SPT–AO–27 If the case file or individual data objects are modified via third–party means then the tool shall provide protection mechanisms disallowing or reporting data modification.
SPT–AO–42 If the cellular forensic tool supports stand–alone acquisition of internal memory with the SIM present, then the contents of the SIM shall not be modified during internal memory acquisition.
SPT–AO–44 If the cellular forensic tool supports acquisition of GPS data then the tool shall present the user with the longitude and latitude coordinates for all GPS–related data

in a useable format.

4 Testing Environment

The tests were run in the NIST CFTT lab. This section describes the testing environment including available computers, mobile devices and the data objects used to populate mobile devices and Subscriber Identity Modules.

4.1 Test Computers

One test computer was used.

Morrisy has the following configuration:

Intel® D975XBX2 Motherboard
BIOS Version BX97520J.86A.2674.2007.0315.1546
Intel® Core™2 Duo CPU 6700 @ 2.66Ghz
3.25 GB RAM
1.44 MB floppy drive
LITE–ON CD H LH52N1P
LITE–ON DVDRW LH–20A1P
2 slots for removable SATA hard disk drive
8 USB 2.0 slots
2 IEEE 1394 ports
3 IEEE 1394 ports (mini)

4.2 Mobile Devices

The following table contains the mobile device used.

Make	Model	OS	Network
Apple iPhone	3G	iPhone	AT&T

4.3 Internal Memory Data Objects

The following data objects were used to populate the internal memory of the smart phones.

Data Objects	Data Elements
Address Book Entries	
	Regular Length
	Maximum Length
	Special Character
	Blank Name
	Regular Length, email
	Regular Length, graphic

Data Objects	Data Elements
	Deleted Entry
	Non–ASCII Entry
PIM Data	
	Regular Length
	Maximum Length
	Deleted Entry
	Special Character
Call Logs	
	Incoming
	Outgoing
	Missed
	Incoming – Deleted
	Outgoing – Deleted
	Missed – Deleted
Text Messages	
	Incoming SMS – Read
	Incoming SMS – Unread
	Outgoing SMS
	Incoming EMS – Read
	Incoming EMS – Unread
	Outgoing EMS
	Incoming SMS – Deleted
	Outgoing SMS – Deleted
	Incoming EMS – Deleted
	Outgoing EMS – Deleted
	Non–ASCII EMS
MMS Messages	
	Incoming Audio
	Incoming Graphic
	Incoming Video
	Outgoing Audio
	Outgoing Graphic
	Outgoing Video
Stand–alone data files	
	Audio
	Graphic
	Video
	Audio – Deleted
	Graphic – Deleted
	Video – Deleted
Application Data	
	Device Specific App Data
Location Data	
	GPS Coordinates

4.4 Subscriber Identity Module Data Objects

The following data objects were used to populate the Subscriber Identity Modules.

Data Objects	Data Elements
Abbreviated Dialing Numbers (ADN)	
	Maximum Length
	Special Character
	Blank Name
	Non–ASCII Entry
	Regular Length – Deleted Number
Call Logs	
	Last Numbers Dialed (LND)
Text Messages	
	Incoming SMS – Read
	Incoming SMS – Unread
	Non–ASCII SMS
	Incoming SMS – Deleted
	Non–ASCII EMS
	Incoming EMS – Deleted

5 Test Results

The main item of interest for interpreting the test results is determining the conformance of the tool with the test assertions. Conformance with each assertion tested by a given test case is evaluated by examining the **Results** box of the test case details.

5.1 Test Results Report Key

A summary of the actual test results is presented in this report. The following table presents a description of each section of the test report summary.

Table 5 Test Results Report Key

Heading	Description
First Line:	Test case ID, name, and version of tool tested.
Case Summary:	Test case summary from *Smart Phone Tool Test Assertion and Test Plan.*
Assertions:	The test assertions applicable to the test case, selected from *Smart Phone Tool Test Assertion and Test Plan.*
Tester Name:	Name or initials of person executing test procedure.
Test Host:	Host computer executing the test.
Test Date:	Time and date that test was started.
Device:	Source mobile device, media (i.e., SIM).

Heading	Description
Source Setup:	Acquisition interface.
Log Highlights:	Information extracted from various log files to illustrate conformance or non–conformance to the test assertions.
Results:	Expected and actual results for each assertion tested.
Analysis:	Whether or not the expected results were achieved.

5.2 Test Details

5.2.1 SPT–01 (iPhone 3G)

Test Case SPT-01 iXAM 1.5.6 iXAMiner 2.3	
Case Summary:	SPT-01 Acquire mobile device internal memory over tool-supported interfaces (e.g., cable, Bluetooth, IrDA).
Assertions:	SPT-CA-01 If a cellular forensic tool provides support for connectivity of the target device then the tool shall successfully recognize the target device via all vendor supported interfaces (e.g., cable, Bluetooth, IrDA). SPT-CA-04 If a cellular forensic tool completes acquisition of the target device without error then the tool shall have the ability to present acquired data objects in a useable format via either a preview-pane or generated report. SPT-CA-30 If a cellular forensic tool provides the user with a "Select All" individual device data objects then the tool shall complete the acquisition of all individually selected data objects without error. SPT-CA-32 If a cellular forensic tool completes two consecutive logical acquisitions of the target device without error then the payload (data objects) on the mobile device shall remain consistent.
Tester Name:	rpa
Test Host:	Morrisy
Test Date:	Thu Aug 12 10:14:09 EDT 2010
Device:	iPhone3G
Source Setup:	OS: WIN XP Interface: cable
Log Highlights:	Created by iXAM 1.5.6 Acquisition started: Thu Aug 12 10:14:09 EDT 2010 Acquisition finished: Thu Aug 12 10:38:34 EDT 2010 Device connectivity was established via supported interface
Results:	

Assertion & Expected Result	Actual Result
SPT-CA-01 Device connectivity via supported interfaces.	as expected
SPT-CA-04 Readability and completeness of acquired data via supported reports.	as expected
SPT-CA-30 Select-All data objects acquisition.	as expected
SPT-CA-32 Perform back-to-back acquisitions, check device payload for modifications.	as expected

Analysis:	Expected results achieved

5.2.2 SPT–02 (iPhone 3G)

Test Case SPT-02 iXAM 1.5.6 iXAMiner 2.3	
Case Summary:	SPT-02 Attempt internal memory acquisition of a non-supported mobile device.
Assertions:	SPT-CA-02 If a cellular forensic tool attempts to connect to a non-supported device then the tool shall notify the user that the device is not supported.
Tester Name:	rpa
Test Host:	Morrisy
Test Date:	Thu Aug 12 10:40:47 EDT 2010
Device:	unsupported device
Source Setup:	OS: WIN XP Interface: cable
Log Highlights:	Created by iXAM 1.5.6 Acquisition started: Thu Aug 12 10:40:47 EDT 2010 Acquisition finished: Thu Aug 12 10:45:06 EDT 2010 Identification of non-supported devices was successful
Results:	

Assertion & Expected Result	Actual Result
SPT-CA-02 Identification of non-supported devices.	as expected

Analysis:	Expected results achieved

5.2.3 SPT–03 (iPhone 3G)

Test Case SPT-03 iXAM 1.5.6 iXAMiner 2.3	
Case Summary:	SPT-03 Begin mobile device internal memory acquisition and interrupt connectivity by interface disengagement.
Assertions:	SPT-CA-03 If connectivity between the mobile device and cellular forensic tool is disrupted then the tool shall notify the user that connectivity has been disrupted.
Tester Name:	rpa
Test Host:	Morrisy
Test Date:	Thu Aug 12 10:46:08 EDT 2010
Device:	iPhone3G
Source Setup:	OS: WIN XP Interface: cable
Log Highlights:	Created by iXAM 1.5.6 Acquisition started: Thu Aug 12 10:46:08 EDT 2010 Acquisition finished: Thu Aug 12 10:59:01 EDT 2010 Device acquisition disruption notification was successful

Results:	Assertion & Expected Result	Actual Result
	SPT-CA-03 Notification of device acquisition disruption.	as expected

Analysis:	Expected results achieved

5.2.4 SPT–04 (iPhone 3G)

Test Case SPT-04 iXAM 1.5.6 iXAMiner 2.3	
Case Summary:	SPT-04 Acquire mobile device internal memory and review reported data via the preview-pane or generated reports for readability.
Assertions:	SPT-CA-04 If a cellular forensic tool completes acquisition of the target device without error then the tool shall have the ability to present acquired data objects in a useable format via either a preview-pane or generated report.
Tester Name:	rpa
Test Host:	Morrisy
Test Date:	Thu Aug 12 10:59:45 EDT 2010
Device:	iPhone3G
Source Setup:	OS: WIN XP Interface: cable
Log Highlights:	Created by iXAM 1.5.6 Acquisition started: Thu Aug 12 10:59:45 EDT 2010 Acquisition finished: Thu Aug 12 11:03:25 EDT 2010 Readability and completeness of acquired data was successful
Results:	

Assertion & Expected Result	Actual Result
SPT-CA-04 Readability and completeness of acquired data via supported reports.	as expected

Analysis:	Expected results achieved

5.2.5 SPT–05 (iPhone 3G)

Test Case SPT-05 iXAM 1.5.6 iXAMiner 2.3	
Case Summary:	SPT-05 Acquire mobile device internal memory and review reported subscriber and equipment related information (e.g., IMEI/MEID/ESN, MSISDN).
Assertions:	SPT-CA-05 If a cellular forensic tool completes acquisition of the target device without error then subscriber-related information shall be presented in a useable format. SPT-CA-06 If a cellular forensic tool completes acquisition of the target device without error then equipment related information shall be presented in a useable format.
Tester Name:	rpa
Test Host:	Morrisy
Test Date:	Thu Aug 12 11:03:49 EDT 2010
Device:	iPhone
Source Setup:	OS: WIN XP Interface: cable
Log Highlights:	Created by iXAM 1.5.6 Acquisition started: Thu Aug 12 11:03:49 EDT 2010 Acquisition finished: Thu Aug 12 11:07:09 EDT 2010 Subscriber and Equipment related data (i.e., MSISDN, IMEI) were acquired
Results:	

Assertion & Expected Result	Actual Result
SPT-CA-05 Acquisition of MSISDN, IMSI.	as expected
SPT-CA-06 Acquisition of IMEI/MEID/ESN.	as expected

Analysis:	Expected results achieved

5.2.6 SPT–06 (iPhone 3G)

Test Case SPT-06 iXAM 1.5.6 iXAMiner 2.3	
Case Summary:	SPT-06 Acquire mobile device internal memory and review reported PIM related data.
Assertions:	SPT-CA-07 If a cellular forensic tool completes acquisition of the target device without error then address book entries shall be presented in a useable format. SPT-CA-08 If a cellular forensic tool completes acquisition of the target device without error then maximum length address book entries shall be presented in a useable format. SPT-CA-09 If a cellular forensic tool completes acquisition of the target device without error then address book entries containing special characters shall be presented in a useable format. SPT-CA-10 If a cellular forensic tool completes acquisition of the target device without error then address book entries containing blank names shall be presented in a useable format. SPT-CA-11 If a cellular forensic tool completes acquisition of the target device without error then email addresses associated with address book entries shall be presented in a useable format. SPT-CA-12 If a cellular forensic tool completes acquisition of the target device without error then graphics associated with address book entries shall be presented in a useable format. SPT-CA-13 If a cellular forensic tool completes acquisition of the target device without error then datebook, calendar, note entries shall be presented in a useable format. SPT-CA-14 If a cellular forensic tool completes acquisition of the target device without error then maximum length datebook, calendar, note entries shall be presented in a useable format.
Tester Name:	rpa
Test Host:	Morrisy
Test Date:	Thu Aug 12 11:08:09 EDT 2010
Device:	iPhone3G
Source Setup:	OS: WIN XP Interface: cable
Log Highlights:	Created by iXAM 1.5.6 Acquisition started: Thu Aug 12 11:08:09 EDT 2010 Acquisition finished: Thu Aug 12 11:12:13 EDT 2010 All address book entries were successfully acquired ALL PIM related data was acquired
Results:	(table below)

Assertion & Expected Result	Actual Result
SPT-CA-07 Acquisition of address book entries.	as expected
SPT-CA-08 Acquisition of maximum length address book entries.	as expected
SPT-CA-09 Acquisition of address book entries containing special characters.	as expected
SPT-CA-10 Acquisition of address book entries containing a blank name entry.	as expected
SPT-CA-11 Acquisition of embedded email addresses within address book entries.	as expected
SPT-CA-12 Acquisition of embedded graphics within address book entries.	as expected
SPT-CA-13 Acquisition of PIM data (i.e., datebook/calendar, notes).	as expected
SPT-CA-14 Acquisition of maximum length PIM data.	as expected

Analysis:	Expected results achieved

5.2.7 SPT–07 (iPhone 3G)

Test Case SPT-07 iXAM 1.5.6 iXAMiner 2.3	
Case Summary:	SPT-07 Acquire mobile device internal memory and review reported call logs.
Assertions:	SPT-CA-15 If a cellular forensic tool completes acquisition of the target device without error then call logs (incoming/outgoing/missed) shall be presented in a useable format. SPT-CA-16 If a cellular forensic tool completes acquisition of the target device without error then the corresponding date/time stamps and the duration of the call for call logs shall be presented in a useable format.
Tester Name:	rpa
Test Host:	Morrisy
Test Date:	Thu Aug 12 11:15:34 EDT 2010
Device:	iPhone3G
Source Setup:	OS: WIN XP Interface: cable
Log Highlights:	Created by iXAM 1.5.6 Acquisition started: Thu Aug 12 11:15:34 EDT 2010 Acquisition finished: Thu Aug 12 11:16:57 EDT 2010 All Call Logs (incoming, outgoing, missed) were acquired All Call Log date/time stamps data were correctly reported
Results:	

Assertion & Expected Result	Actual Result
SPT-CA-15 Acquisition of call logs.	as expected
SPT-CA-16 Acquisition of call log date/time stamps.	as expected

Analysis:	Expected results achieved

5.2.8 SPT–08 (iPhone 3G)

Test Case SPT-08 iXAM 1.5.6 iXAMiner 2.3	
Case Summary:	SPT-08 Acquire mobile device internal memory and review reported text messages.
Assertions:	SPT-CA-17 If a cellular forensic tool completes acquisition of the target device without error then ASCII text messages (i.e., SMS, EMS) shall be presented in a useable format. SPT-CA-18 If a cellular forensic tool completes acquisition of the target device without error then the corresponding date/time stamps for text messages shall be presented in a useable format. SPT-CA-19 If a cellular forensic tool completes acquisition of the target device without error then the corresponding status (i.e., read, unread) for text messages shall be presented in a useable format. SPT-CA-20 If a cellular forensic tool completes acquisition of the target device without error then the corresponding sender / recipient phone numbers for text messages shall be presented in a useable format.
Tester Name:	rpa
Test Host:	Morrisy
Test Date:	Thu Aug 12 11:19:03 EDT 2010
Device:	iPhone3G
Source Setup:	OS: WIN XP Interface: cable
Log Highlights:	Created by iXAM 1.5.6 Acquisition started: Thu Aug 12 11:19:03 EDT 2010 Acquisition finished: Thu Aug 12 11:21:41 EDT 2010 ALL text messages (SMS, EMS) were acquired Correct date/time stamps were reported for all text messages Correct status flags were reported for all text messages Sender and Recipient phone numbers associated with text messages were correctly reported

Results:	Assertion & Expected Result	Actual Result
	SPT-CA-17 Acquisition of text messages.	as expected
	SPT-CA-18 Acquisition of text message date/time stamps.	as expected
	SPT-CA-19 Acquisition of text message status flags.	as expected
	SPT-CA-20 Acquisition of sender/recipient phone number associated with text messages.	as expected

Analysis:	Expected results achieved

5.2.9 SPT–09 (iPhone 3G)

Test Case SPT-09 iXAM 1.5.6 iXAMiner 2.3	
Case Summary:	SPT-09 Acquire mobile device internal memory and review reported MMS multi-media related data (i.e., text, audio, graphics, video).
Assertions:	SPT-CA-21 If a cellular forensic tool completes acquisition of the target device without error then MMS messages and associated audio shall be presented in a useable format. SPT-CA-22 If a cellular forensic tool completes acquisition of the target device without error then MMS messages and associated graphic files shall be presented in a useable format. SPT-CA-23 If a cellular forensic tool completes acquisition of the target device without error then MMS messages and associated video shall be presented in a useable format.
Tester Name:	rpa
Test Host:	Morrisy
Test Date:	Thu Aug 12 11:25:46 EDT 2010
Device:	iPhone3G
Source Setup:	OS: WIN XP Interface: cable
Log Highlights:	Created by iXAM 1.5.6 Acquisition started: Thu Aug 12 11:25:46 EDT 2010 Acquisition finished: Thu Aug 12 11:27:00 EDT 2010 ALL MMS messages (Audio, Image, Video) were acquired
Results:	<table><tr><th>Assertion & Expected Result</th><th>Actual Result</th></tr><tr><td>SPT-CA-21 Acquisition of audio MMS messages.</td><td>as expected</td></tr><tr><td>SPT-CA-22 Acquisition of graphic data image MMS messages.</td><td>as expected</td></tr><tr><td>SPT-CA-23 Acquisition of video MMS messages.</td><td>as expected</td></tr></table>
Analysis:	Expected results achieved

5.2.10 SPT–10 (iPhone 3G)

Test Case SPT-10 iXAM 1.5.6 iXAMiner 2.3	
Case Summary:	SPT-10 Acquire mobile device internal memory and review reported stand-alone multi-media data (i.e., audio, graphics, video).
Assertions:	SPT-CA-24 If a cellular forensic tool completes acquisition of the target device without error then stand-alone audio files shall be presented in a useable format via either an internal application or suggested third-party application. SPT-CA-25 If a cellular forensic tool completes acquisition of the target device without error then stand-alone graphic files shall be presented in a useable format via either an internal application or suggested third-party application. SPT-CA-26 If a cellular forensic tool completes acquisition of the target device without error then stand-alone video files shall be presented in a useable format via either an internal application or suggested third-party application.
Tester Name:	rpa
Test Host:	Morrisy
Test Date:	Thu Aug 12 13:14:24 EDT 2010
Device:	iPhone3G
Source Setup:	OS: WIN XP Interface: cable
Log Highlights:	Created by iXAM 1.5.6 Acquisition started: Thu Aug 12 13:14:24 EDT 2010 Acquisition finished: Thu Aug 12 13:18:11 EDT 2010 ALL stand-alone data files (Audio, Image, Video) were acquired
Results:	<table><tr><th>Assertion & Expected Result</th><th>Actual Result</th></tr><tr><td>SPT-CA-24 Acquisition of stand-alone audio files.</td><td>as expected</td></tr><tr><td>SPT-CA-25 Acquisition of stand-alone graphic files.</td><td>as expected</td></tr><tr><td>SPT-CA-26 Acquisition of stand-alone video files.</td><td>as expected</td></tr></table>
Analysis:	Expected results achieved

5.2.11 SPT–11 (iPhone 3G)

Test Case SPT-11 iXAM 1.5.6 iXAMiner 2.3	
Case Summary:	SPT-11 Acquire mobile device internal memory and review application related data (i.e., word documents, spreadsheet, presentation documents).
Assertions:	SPT-CA-27 If a cellular forensic tool completes acquisition of the target device without error then device specific application related data shall be acquired and presented in a useable format via either an internal application or suggested third-party application.
Tester Name:	rpa
Test Host:	Morrisy
Test Date:	Thu Aug 12 13:27:25 EDT 2010
Device:	iPhone3G
Source Setup:	OS: WIN XP Interface: cable
Log Highlights:	Created by iXAM 1.5.6 Acquisition started: Thu Aug 12 13:27:25 EDT 2010 Acquisition finished: Thu Aug 12 13:33:34 EDT 2010 All application data was acquired
Results:	

Assertion & Expected Result	Actual Result
SPT-CA-27 Acquisition of application related data.	as expected

Analysis:	Expected results achieved

5.2.12 SPT-12 (iPhone 3G)

Test Case SPT-12 iXAM 1.5.6 iXAMiner 2.3	
Case Summary:	SPT-12 Acquire mobile device internal memory and review Internet related data (i.e., bookmarks, visited sites.
Assertions:	SPT-CA-28 If a cellular forensic tool completes acquisition of the target device without error then Internet related data (i.e., bookmarks, visited sites) cached to the device shall be acquired and presented in a useable format.
Tester Name:	rpa
Test Host:	Morrisy
Test Date:	Thu Aug 12 13:57:57 EDT 2010
Device:	iPhone3G
Source Setup:	OS: WIN XP Interface: cable
Log Highlights:	Created by iXAM 1.5.6 Acquisition started: Thu Aug 12 13:57:57 EDT 2010 Acquisition finished: Thu Aug 12 13:58:46 EDT 2010 All Internet related data was acquired
Results:	

Assertion & Expected Result	Actual Result
SPT-CA-28 Acquisition of Internet related data.	as expected

Analysis:	Expected results achieved

5.2.13 SPT–13 (iPhone 3G)

Test Case SPT-13 iXAM 1.5.6 iXAMiner 2.3	
Case Summary:	SPT-13 Acquire mobile device internal memory by selecting a combination of supported data elements.
Assertions:	SPT-CA-30 If a cellular forensic tool provides the user with an "Select All" individual device data objects then the tool shall complete the acquisition of all individually selected data objects without error.
Tester Name:	rpa
Test Host:	Morrisy
Test Date:	Thu Aug 12 14:00:28 EDT 2010
Device:	iPhone3G
Source Setup:	OS: WIN XP Interface: cable
Log Highlights:	Created by iXAM 1.5.6 Acquisition started: Thu Aug 12 14:00:28 EDT 2010 Acquisition finished: Thu Aug 12 14:02:21 EDT 2010 Select All acquisition was successful
Results:	

Assertion & Expected Result	Actual Result
SPT-CA-30 Select-All data objects acquisition.	as expected

Analysis:	Expected results achieved

5.2.14 SPT–14 (iPhone 3G)

Test Case SPT-14 iXAM 1.5.6 iXAMiner 2.3	
Case Summary:	SPT-14 Acquire SIM memory over supported interfaces (e.g., PC/SC reader).
Assertions:	SPT-AO-01 If a cellular forensic tool provides support for connectivity of the target SIM then the tool shall successfully recognize the target SIM via all tool-supported interfaces (e.g., PC/SC reader, proprietary reader, smart phone itself).
Tester Name:	rpa
Test Host:	Morrisy
Test Date:	Thu Aug 12 14:37:10 EDT 2010
Device:	ATT SIM
Source Setup:	OS: WIN XP Interface: USB
Log Highlights:	Created by iXAM 1.5.6 Acquisition started: Thu Aug 12 14:37:10 EDT 2010 Acquisition finished: Thu Aug 12 14:39:29 EDT 2010 Media connectivity was established via supported interface

Results:	Assertion & Expected Result	Actual Result
	SPT-AO-01 SIM connectivity via supported interfaces.	as expected

Analysis:	Expected results achieved

5.2.15 SPT–15 (iPhone 3G)

Test Case SPT-15 iXAM 1.5.6 iXAMiner 2.3	
Case Summary:	SPT-15 Attempt acquisition of a non-supported SIM.
Assertions:	SPT-AO-02 If a cellular forensic tool attempts to connect to a non-supported SIM then the tool shall notify the user that the SIM is not supported.
Tester Name:	rpa
Test Host:	Morrisy
Test Date:	Thu Aug 12 14:40:23 EDT 2010
Device:	ATT SIM
Source Setup:	OS: WIN XP Interface: USB
Log Highlights:	Created by iXAM 1.5.6 Acquisition started: Thu Aug 12 14:40:23 EDT 2010 Acquisition finished: Thu Aug 12 14:44:31 EDT 2010 Identification of non-supported media was successful
Results:	<table><tr><td>**Assertion & Expected Result**</td><td>**Actual Result**</td></tr><tr><td>SPT-AO-02 Identification of non-supported SIMs.</td><td>as expected</td></tr></table>
Analysis:	Expected results achieved

5.2.16 SPT–16 (iPhone 3G)

Test Case SPT-16 iXAM 1.5.6 iXAMiner 2.3	
Case Summary:	SPT-16 Begin SIM acquisition and interrupt connectivity by interface disengagement.
Assertions:	SPT-AO-03 If a cellular forensic tool loses connectivity with the SIM reader then the tool shall notify the user that connectivity has been disrupted.
Tester Name:	rpa
Test Host:	Morrisy
Test Date:	Thu Aug 12 14:44:57 EDT 2010
Device:	ATT SIM
Source Setup:	OS: WIN XP Interface: USB
Log Highlights:	Created by iXAM 1.5.6 Acquisition started: Thu Aug 12 14:44:57 EDT 2010 Acquisition finished: Thu Aug 12 14:47:41 EDT 2010 Media acquisition disruption notification was successful
Results:	<table><tr><th>Assertion & Expected Result</th><th>Actual Result</th></tr><tr><td>SPT-AO-03 Notification of SIM acquisition disruption.</td><td>as expected</td></tr></table>
Analysis:	Expected results achieved

5.2.17 SPT–17 (iPhone 3G)

Test Case SPT-17 iXAM 1.5.6 iXAMiner 2.3	
Case Summary:	SPT-17 Acquire SIM memory and review reported subscriber and equipment related information (i.e., SPN, ICCID, IMSI, MSISDN).
Assertions:	SPT-AO-04 If a cellular forensic tool completes acquisition of the target SIM without error then the SPN shall be presented in a useable format. SPT-AO-05 If a cellular forensic tool completes acquisition of the target SIM without error then the ICCID shall be presented in a useable format. SPT-AO-06 If a cellular forensic tool completes acquisition of the target SIM without error then the IMSI shall be presented in a useable format. SPT-AO-07 If a cellular forensic tool completes acquisition of the target SIM without error then the MSISDN shall be presented in a useable format.
Tester Name:	rpa
Test Host:	Morrisy
Test Date:	Thu Aug 12 14:48:04 EDT 2010
Device:	ATT_SIM
Source Setup:	OS: WIN XP Interface: USB
Log Highlights:	Created by iXAM 1.5.6 Acquisition started: Thu Aug 12 14:48:04 EDT 2010 Acquisition finished: Thu Aug 12 14:55:04 EDT 2010 All subscriber-related data (i.e., SPN, ICCID, IMSI, MSISDN) was acquired
Results:	<table><tr><th>Assertion & Expected Result</th><th>Actual Result</th></tr><tr><td>SPT-AO-04 Acquisition of SPN.</td><td>as expected</td></tr><tr><td>SPT-AO-05 Acquisition of ICCID.</td><td>as expected</td></tr><tr><td>SPT-AO-06 Acquisition of IMSI.</td><td>as expected</td></tr><tr><td>SPT-AO-07 Acquisition of MSISDN.</td><td>as expected</td></tr></table>
Analysis:	Expected results achieved

5.2.18 SPT–18 (iPhone 3G)

Test Case SPT-18 iXAM 1.5.6 iXAMiner 2.3	
Case Summary:	SPT-18 Acquire SIM memory and review reported Abbreviated Dialing Numbers (ADN).
Assertions:	SPT-AO-08 If a cellular forensic tool completes acquisition of the target SIM without error then ASCII Abbreviated Dialing Numbers (ADN) shall be presented in a useable format. SPT-AO-09 If a cellular forensic tool completes acquisition of the target SIM without error then maximum length ADNs shall be presented in a useable format. SPT-AO-10 If a cellular forensic tool completes acquisition of the SIM without error then ADNs containing special characters shall be presented in a useable format. SPT-AO-11 If a cellular forensic tool completes acquisition of the SIM without error then ADNs containing blank names shall be presented in a useable format.
Tester Name:	rpa
Test Host:	Morrisy
Test Date:	Thu Aug 12 14:55:35 EDT 2010
Device:	ATT SIM
Source Setup:	OS: WIN XP Interface: cable
Log Highlights:	Created by iXAM 1.5.6 Acquisition started: Thu Aug 12 14:55:35 EDT 2010 Acquisition finished: Thu Aug 12 14:58:39 EDT 2010 All ADNs were acquired
Results:	

Assertion & Expected Result	Actual Result
SPT-AO-08 Acquisition of ADNs.	as expected
SPT-AO-09 Acquisition of maximum length ADNs.	as expected
SPT-AO-10 Acquisition of special character ADNs.	as expected
SPT-AO-11 Acquisition of blank name ADNs.	as expected

Analysis:	Expected results achieved

5.2.19 SPT–19 (iPhone 3G)

Test Case SPT-19 iXAM 1.5.6 iXAMiner 2.3	
Case Summary:	SPT-19 Acquire SIM memory and review reported Last Numbers Dialed (LND).
Assertions:	SPT-AO-12 If a cellular forensic tool completes acquisition of the target SIM without error then Last Numbers Dialed (LND) shall be presented in a useable format. SPT-AO-13 If a cellular forensic tool completes acquisition of the target SIM without error then the corresponding date/time stamps for LNDs shall be presented in a useable format.
Tester Name:	rpa
Test Host:	Morrisy
Test Date:	Thu Aug 12 14:59:17 EDT 2010
Device:	ATT_SIM
Source Setup:	OS: WIN XP Interface: USB
Log Highlights:	Created by iXAM 1.5.6 Acquisition started: Thu Aug 12 14:59:17 EDT 2010 Acquisition finished: Thu Aug 12 15:00:57 EDT 2010 LNDs were acquired Date/Time Stamps correctly reported for LNDs
Results:	

Assertion & Expected Result	Actual Result
SPT-AO-12 Acquisition of LNDs.	as expected
SPT-AO-13 Acquisition of LND date/time stamps.	as expected

Analysis:	Expected results achieved

5.2.20 SPT–20 (iPhone 3G)

Test Case SPT-20 iXAM 1.5.6 iXAMiner 2.3	
Case Summary:	SPT-20 Acquire SIM memory and review reported text messages (SMS, EMS).
Assertions:	SPT-AO-14 If a cellular forensic tool completes acquisition of the target SIM without error then ASCII SMS text messages shall be presented in a useable format. SPT-AO-15 If a cellular forensic tool completes acquisition of the target SIM without error then ASCII EMS text messages shall be presented in a useable format. SPT-AO-16 If a cellular forensic tool completes acquisition of the target SIM without error then the corresponding date/time stamps for all text messages shall be presented in a useable format. SPT-AO-17 If a cellular forensic tool completes acquisition of the target SIM without error then the corresponding status (i.e., read, unread) for text messages shall be presented in a useable format. SPT-AO-18 If a cellular forensic tool completes acquisition of the target SIM without error then the corresponding sender / recipient phone numbers for text messages shall be presented in a useable format.
Tester Name:	rpa
Test Host:	Morrisy
Test Date:	Thu Aug 12 15:01:21 EDT 2010
Device:	ATT_SIM
Source Setup:	OS: WIN XP Interface: USB
Log Highlights:	Created by iXAM 1.5.6 Acquisition started: Thu Aug 12 15:01:21 EDT 2010 Acquisition finished: Thu Aug 12 15:04:10 EDT 2010 ALL text messages (SMS, EMS) were acquired All date/time stamps were reported for text messages Correct status flags were reported for text messages Sender and Recipient phone numbers associated with text messages were correctly reported
Results:	<table><tr><th>Assertion & Expected Result</th><th>Actual Result</th></tr><tr><td>SPT-AO-14 Acquisition of SMS messages.</td><td>as expected</td></tr><tr><td>SPT-AO-15 Acquisition of EMS messages.</td><td>as expected</td></tr><tr><td>SPT-AO-16 Acquisition of text message date/time stamps.</td><td>as expected</td></tr><tr><td>SPT-AO-17 Acquisition of text message status flags.</td><td>as expected</td></tr><tr><td>SPT-AO-18 Acquisition of sender/recipient phone number associated with text messages.</td><td>as expected</td></tr></table>
Analysis:	Expected results achieved

5.2.21 SPT–21 (iPhone 3G)

Test Case SPT-21 iXAM 1.5.6 iXAMiner 2.3	
Case Summary:	SPT-21 Acquire SIM memory and review recoverable deleted text messages (SMS, EMS).
Assertions:	SPT-AO-19 If the cellular forensic tool completes acquisition of the target SIM without error then deleted text messages that have not been overwritten shall be presented in a useable format.
Tester Name:	rpa
Test Host:	Morrisy
Test Date:	Thu Aug 12 15:04:34 EDT 2010
Device:	ATT SIM
Source Setup:	OS: WIN XP Interface: USB
Log Highlights:	Created by iXAM 1.5.6 Acquisition started: Thu Aug 12 15:04:34 EDT 2010 Acquisition finished: Thu Aug 12 15:11:38 EDT 2010 Deleted text message data was recovered
Results:	

Assertion & Expected Result	Actual Result
SPT-AO-19 Acquisition of non-overwritten deleted text messages.	as expected

Analysis:	Expected results achieved

5.2.22 SPT–22 (iPhone 3G)

Test Case SPT-22 iXAM 1.5.6 iXAMiner 2.3	
Case Summary:	SPT-22 Acquire SIM memory and review reported location related data (i.e., LOCI, GPRSLOCI).
Assertions:	SPT-AO-20 If a cellular forensic tool completes acquisition of the target SIM without error then location related data (i.e., LOCI) shall be presented in a useable format. SPT-AO-21 If a cellular forensic tool completes acquisition of the target SIM without error then location related data (i.e., GRPSLOCI) shall be presented in a useable format.
Tester Name:	rpa
Test Host:	Morrisy
Test Date:	Thu Aug 12 15:14:11 EDT 2010
Device:	ATT_SIM
Source Setup:	OS: WIN XP Interface: USB
Log Highlights:	Created by iXAM 1.5.6 Acquisition started: Thu Aug 12 15:14:11 EDT 2010 Acquisition finished: Thu Aug 12 15:14:49 EDT 2010 LOCI data was acquired GPRSLOCI data was acquired
Results:	<table><tr><td>Assertion & Expected Result</td><td>Actual Result</td></tr><tr><td>SPT-AO-20 Acquisition of LOCI information.</td><td>as expected</td></tr><tr><td>SPT-AO-21 Acquisition of GPRSLOCI information.</td><td>as expected</td></tr></table>
Analysis:	Expected results achieved

5.2.23 SPT–23 (iPhone 3G)

Test Case SPT–23 iXAM 1.5.6 iXAMiner 2.3	
Case Summary:	SPT-23 Acquire SIM memory by selecting a combination of supported data elements.
Assertions:	SPT-AO-01 If a cellular forensic tool provides support for connectivity of the target SIM then the tool shall successfully recognize the target SIM via all tool-supported interfaces (e.g., PC/SC reader, proprietary reader, smart phone itself). SPT-AO-23 If a cellular forensic tool provides the user with an "Select All" individual SIM data objects then the tool shall complete the acquisition of all individually selected data objects without error.
Tester Name:	rpa
Test Host:	Morrisy
Test Date:	Thu Aug 12 15:15:07 EDT 2010
Device:	ATT_SIM
Source Setup:	OS: WIN XP Interface: USB
Log Highlights:	Created by iXAM 1.5.6 Acquisition started: Thu Aug 12 15:15:07 EDT 2010 Acquisition finished: Thu Aug 12 15:15:17 EDT 2010 Select All acquisition was successful
Results:	

Assertion & Expected Result	Actual Result
SPT-AO-01 SIM connectivity via supported interfaces.	as expected
SPT-AO-23 Select-All data objects acquisition.	as expected

Analysis:	Expected results achieved

5.2.24 SPT–24 (iPhone 3G)

Test Case SPT-24 iXAM 1.5.6 iXAMiner 2.3	
Case Summary:	SPT-24 Acquire mobile device internal memory and review reported data via supported generated report formats.
Assertions:	SPT-AO-25 If a cellular forensic tool completes acquisition of the target device without error then the tool shall present the acquired data in a useable format via supported generated report formats.
Tester Name:	rpa
Test Host:	Morrisy
Test Date:	Fri Aug 13 07:45:26 EDT 2010
Device:	iPhone3G
Source Setup:	OS: WIN XP Interface: cable
Log Highlights:	Created by iXAM 1.5.6 Acquisition started: Fri Aug 13 07:45:26 EDT 2010 Acquisition finished: Fri Aug 13 07:46:36 EDT 2010 Complete representation of known data via generated reports was successful
Results:	

Assertion & Expected Result	Actual Result
SPT-AO-25 Comparison of known device data elements via generated reports.	as expected

Analysis:	Expected results achieved

5.2.25 SPT–26 (iPhone 3G)

Test Case SPT–26 iXAM 1.5.6 iXAMiner 2.3	
Case Summary:	SPT-26 Acquire SIM memory and review reported data via supported generated report formats.
Assertions:	SPT-AO-25 If a cellular forensic tool completes acquisition of the SIM without error then the tool shall present the acquired data in a useable format via supported generated report formats.
Tester Name:	rpa
Test Host:	Morrisy
Test Date:	Fri Aug 13 07:46:57 EDT 2010
Device:	ATT SIM
Source Setup:	OS: WIN XP Interface: USB
Log Highlights:	Created by iXAM 1.5.6 Acquisition started: Fri Aug 13 07:46:57 EDT 2010 Acquisition finished: Fri Aug 13 07:50:03 EDT 2010 Complete representation of known data via generated reports was successful
Results:	

Assertion & Expected Result	Actual Result
SPT-AO-25 Comparison of known device data elements via generated reports.	as expected

Analysis:	Expected results achieved

5.2.26 SPT–28 (iPhone 3G)

Test Case SPT–28 iXAM 1.5.6 iXAMiner 2.3	
Case Summary:	SPT–28 Attempt acquisition of a password-protected SIM.
Assertions:	SPT-AO-28 If the SIM is password-protected then the cellular forensic tool shall provide the examiner with the opportunity to input the PIN before acquisition.
Tester Name:	rpa
Test Host:	Morrisy
Test Date:	Fri Aug 13 07:50:29 EDT 2010
Device:	ATT SIM
Source Setup:	OS: WIN XP Interface: USB
Log Highlights:	Created by iXAM 1.5.6 Acquisition started: Fri Aug 13 07:50:29 EDT 2010 Acquisition finished: Fri Aug 13 07:56:28 EDT 2010 Ability to enter PIN on protected media before acquisition was successful
Results:	

Assertion & Expected Result	Actual Result
SPT-AO-28 Acquisition of password protected SIM.	as expected

Analysis:	Expected results achieved

5.2.27 SPT–31 (iPhone 3G)

Test Case SPT–31 iXAM 1.5.6 iXAMiner 2.3	
Case Summary:	SPT-31 Perform a physical acquisition and review data output for readability.
Assertions:	SPT-AO-31 If the cellular forensic tool supports a physical acquisition of the target device then the tool shall complete the acquisition without error.
Tester Name:	rpa
Test Host:	Morrisy
Test Date:	Fri Aug 13 10:32:49 EDT 2010
Device:	iPhone3G
Source Setup:	OS: WIN XP Interface: cable
Log Highlights:	Created by iXAM 1.5.6 Acquisition started: Fri Aug 13 10:32:49 EDT 2010 Acquisition finished: Fri Aug 13 12:35:21 EDT 2010 Physical Acquisition: readability and completeness was successful
Results:	

Assertion & Expected Result	Actual Result
SPT-AO-31 Physical acquisition, data is presented in a useable format.	as expected

Analysis:	Expected results achieved

5.2.28 SPT–32 (iPhone 3G)

Test Case SPT-32 iXAM 1.5.6 iXAMiner 2.3	
Case Summary:	SPT–32 Perform a physical acquisition and review reports for recoverable deleted data.
Assertions:	SPT–AO-32 If the cellular forensic tool supports the interpretation of address book entries present on the target device then the tool shall report recoverable active and deleted data or address book data remnants in a useable format. SPT–AO-33 If the cellular forensic tool supports the interpretation of calendar, tasks, or notes present on the target device then the tool shall report recoverable active and deleted calendar, tasks, or note data remnants in a useable format. SPT–AO-34 If the cellular forensic tool supports the interpretation of call logs present on the target device then the tool shall report recoverable active and deleted call or call log data remnants in a useable format. SPT–AO-35 If the cellular forensic tool supports the interpretation of SMS messages present on the target device then the tool shall report recoverable active and deleted SMS messages or SMS message data remnants in a useable format. SPT–AO-36 If the cellular forensic tool supports the interpretation of EMS messages present on the target device then the tool shall report recoverable active and deleted EMS messages or EMS message data remnants in a useable format. SPT–AO-37 If the cellular forensic tool supports the interpretation of audio files present on the target device then the tool shall report recoverable active and deleted audio data or audio file data remnants in a useable format. SPT–AO-38 If the cellular forensic tool supports the interpretation of graphic files present on the target device then the tool shall report recoverable active and deleted graphic file data or graphic file data remnants in a useable format. SPT–AO-39 If the cellular forensic tool supports the interpretation of video files present on the target device then the tool shall report recoverable active and deleted video file data or video file data remnants in a useable format.
Tester Name:	rpa
Test Host:	Morrisy
Test Date:	Fri Aug 13 12:35:40 EDT 2010
Device:	iPhone3G
Source Setup:	OS: WIN XP Interface: cable
Log Highlights:	Created by iXAM 1.5.6 Acquisition started: Fri Aug 13 12:35:40 EDT 2010 Acquisition finished: Fri Aug 13 14:45:51 EDT 2010 Deleted address book entries were not recovered Deleted PIM data was recovered Deleted PIM data was not recovered Deleted Call log data was recovered Deleted Call log data was not recovered Deleted text message data was recovered Deleted audio data was not recovered – NA Deleted graphic data was not recovered – NA Deleted video data was not recovered – NA

Results:	Assertion & Expected Result	Actual Result
	SPT–AO-32 Physical acquisition, recovery of deleted address book entries.	as expected
	SPT–AO-33 Physical acquisition, recovery of deleted PIM data.	as expected
	SPT–AO-34 Physical acquisition, recovery of deleted call logs.	as expected
	SPT–AO-35 Physical acquisition, recovery of deleted SMS	as expected

Test Case SPT-32 iXAM 1.5.6 iXAMiner 2.3		
	messages.	
	SPT-AO-36 Physical acquisition, recovery of deleted EMS messages.	as expected
	SPT-AO-37 Physical acquisition, recovery of deleted stand-alone audio files.	NA
	SPT-AO-38 Physical acquisition, recovery of deleted graphic files.	NA
	SPT-AO-39 Physical acquisition, recovery of deleted video files.	NA
Analysis:	Expected results achieved	

5.2.29 SPT–33 (iPhone 3G)

Test Case SPT-33 iXAM 1.5.6 iXAMiner 2.3	
Case Summary:	SPT-33 Acquire mobile device internal memory and review data containing non-ASCII characters.
Assertions:	SPT-AO-40 If the cellular forensic tool supports display of non-ASCII characters then the application should present address book entries in their native format. SPT-AO-41 If the cellular forensic tool supports proper display of non-ASCII characters then the application should present text messages in their native format.
Tester Name:	rpa
Test Host:	Morrisy
Test Date:	Fri Aug 13 14:46:53 EDT 2010
Device:	iPhone3G
Source Setup:	OS: WIN XP Interface: cable
Log Highlights:	Created by iXAM 1.5.6 Acquisition started: Fri Aug 13 14:46:53 EDT 2010 Acquisition finished: Fri Aug 13 14:48:04 EDT 2010 Non-ASCII Address book entries were acquired and properly displayed Non-ASCII text messages were acquired and properly displayed
Results:	

Assertion & Expected Result	Actual Result
SPT-AO-40 Acquisition of non-ASCII address book entries/ADNs.	as expected
SPT-AO-41 Acquisition of non-ASCII text messages.	as expected

Analysis:	Expected results achieved

5.2.30 SPT–34 (iPhone 3G)

Test Case SPT-34 iXAM 1.5.6 iXAMiner 2.3	
Case Summary:	SPT-34 Acquire SIM memory and review data containing non-ASCII characters.
Assertions:	SPT-AO-40 If the cellular forensic tool supports display of non-ASCII characters then the application should present ADNs in their native format. SPT-AO-41 If the cellular forensic tool supports proper display of non-ASCII characters then the application should present text messages in their native format.
Tester Name:	rpa
Test Host:	Morrisy
Test Date:	Fri Aug 13 14:48:22 EDT 2010
Device:	ATT SIM
Source Setup:	OS: WIN XP Interface: USB
Log Highlights:	Created by iXAM 1.5.6 Acquisition started: Fri Aug 13 14:48:22 EDT 2010 Acquisition finished: Fri Aug 13 14:56:23 EDT 2010 Non-ASCII ADNs were acquired and properly displayed Non-ASCII text messages were acquired and properly displayed
Results:	

Assertion & Expected Result	Actual Result
SPT-AO-40 Acquisition of non-ASCII address book entries/ADNs.	as expected
SPT-AO-41 Acquisition of non-ASCII text messages.	as expected

Analysis:	Expected results achieved

5.2.31 SPT–35 (iPhone 3G)

Test Case SPT-35 iXAM 1.5.6 iXAMiner 2.3	
Case Summary:	SPT-35 Begin acquisition on a PIN protected SIM to determine if the tool provides an accurate count of the remaining number of PIN attempts and if the PIN attempts are decremented when entering an incorrect value.
Assertions:	SPT-AO-29 If a cellular forensic tool provides the examiner with the remaining number of authentication attempts then the application should provide an accurate count of the remaining PIN attempts.
Tester Name:	rpa
Test Host:	Morrisy
Test Date:	Fri Aug 13 14:56:51 EDT 2010
Device:	ATT SIM
Source Setup:	OS: WIN XP Interface: USB
Log Highlights:	Created by iXAM 1.5.6 Acquisition started: Fri Aug 13 14:56:51 EDT 2010 Acquisition finished: Fri Aug 13 14:58:10 EDT 2010 The remaining number of PIN attempts were properly displayed
Results:	

Assertion & Expected Result	Actual Result
SPT-AO-29 Display remaining number of PIN attempts.	as expected

Analysis:	Expected results achieved

5.2.32 SPT–36 (iPhone 3G)

Test Case SPT-36 iXAM 1.5.6 iXAMiner 2.3	
Case Summary:	SPT-36 Begin acquisition on a SIM whose PIN attempts have been exhausted to determine if the tool provides an accurate count of the remaining number of PUK attempts and if the PUK attempts are decremented when entering an incorrect value.
Assertions:	SPT-AO-30 If a cellular forensic tool provides the examiner with the remaining number of PUK attempts then the application should provide an accurate count of the remaining PUK attempts.
Tester Name:	rpa
Test Host:	Morrisy
Test Date:	Fri Aug 13 14:58:29 EDT 2010
Device:	ATT SIM
Source Setup:	OS: WIN XP Interface: USB
Log Highlights:	Created by iXAM 1.5.6 Acquisition started: Fri Aug 13 14:58:29 EDT 2010 Acquisition finished: Fri Aug 13 15:00:18 EDT 2010 Remaining number of PUK attempts were properly displayed
Results:	

Assertion & Expected Result	Actual Result
SPT-AO-30 Display remaining number of PUK attempts.	as expected

Analysis:	Expected results achieved

5.2.33 SPT–38 (iPhone 3G)

Test Case SPT-38 iXAM 1.5.6 iXAMiner 2.3	
Case Summary:	SPT-38 Acquire mobile device internal memory and review hash values for vendor supported data objects.
Assertions:	SPT-AO-43 If the cellular forensic tool supports hashing for individual data objects then the tool shall present the user with a hash value for each supported data object.
Tester Name:	rpa
Test Host:	Morrisy
Test Date:	Fri Aug 13 15:00:47 EDT 2010
Device:	iPhone3G
Source Setup:	OS: WIN XP Interface: cable
Log Highlights:	Created by iXAM 1.5.6 Acquisition started: Fri Aug 13 15:00:47 EDT 2010 Acquisition finished: Fri Aug 13 15:01:50 EDT 2010 Hash values were properly reported for individually acquired device data elements

Results:	Assertion & Expected Result	Actual Result
	SPT-AO-43 Acquire data, check known hash values for consistency.	as expected

Analysis:	Expected results achieved

5.2.34 SPT–39 (iPhone 3G)

Test Case SPT-39 iXAM 1.5.6 iXAMiner 2.3	
Case Summary:	SPT-39 Acquire SIM memory and review hash values for vendor supported data objects.
Assertions:	SPT-AO-43 If the cellular forensic tool supports hashing for individual data objects then the tool shall present the user with a hash value for each supported data object.
Tester Name:	rpa
Test Host:	Morrisy
Test Date:	Fri Aug 13 15:02:35 EDT 2010
Device:	ATT SIM
Source Setup:	OS: WIN XP Interface: USB
Log Highlights:	Created by iXAM 1.5.6 Acquisition started: Fri Aug 13 15:02:35 EDT 2010 Acquisition finished: Fri Aug 13 15:03:43 EDT 2010 Hash values were properly reported for individually acquired SIM data elements
Results:	

Assertion & Expected Result	Actual Result
SPT-AO-43 Acquire data, check known hash values for consistency.	as expected

Analysis:	Expected results achieved

About the National Institute of Justice

A component of the Office of Justice Programs, NIJ is the research, development and evaluation agency of the U.S. Department of Justice. NIJ's mission is to advance scientific research, development and evaluation to enhance the administration of justice and public safety. NIJ's principal authorities are derived from the Omnibus Crime Control and Safe Streets Act of 1968, as amended (see 42 U.S.C. §§ 3721–3723).

The NIJ Director is appointed by the President and confirmed by the Senate. The Director establishes the Institute's objectives, guided by the priorities of the Office of Justice Programs, the U.S. Department of Justice, and the needs of the field. The Institute actively solicits the views of criminal justice and other professionals and researchers to inform its search for the knowledge and tools to guide policy and practice.

Strategic Goals

NIJ has seven strategic goals grouped into three categories:

Creating relevant knowledge and tools

1. Partner with state and local practitioners and policymakers to identify social science research and technology needs.
2. Create scientific, relevant, and reliable knowledge—with a particular emphasis on terrorism, violent crime, drugs and crime, cost-effectiveness, and community-based efforts—to enhance the administration of justice and public safety.
3. Develop affordable and effective tools and technologies to enhance the administration of justice and public safety.

Dissemination

4. Disseminate relevant knowledge and information to practitioners and policymakers in an understandable, timely and concise manner.
5. Act as an honest broker to identify the information, tools and technologies that respond to the needs of stakeholders.

Agency management

6. Practice fairness and openness in the research and development process.
7. Ensure professionalism, excellence, accountability, cost-effectiveness and integrity in the management and conduct of NIJ activities and programs.

Program Areas

In addressing these strategic challenges, the Institute is involved in the following program areas: crime control and prevention, including policing; drugs and crime; justice systems and offender behavior, including corrections; violence and victimization; communications and information technologies; critical incident response; investigative and forensic sciences, including DNA; less-than-lethal technologies; officer protection; education and training technologies; testing and standards; technology assistance to law enforcement and corrections agencies; field testing of promising programs; and international crime control.

In addition to sponsoring research and development and technology assistance, NIJ evaluates programs, policies, and technologies. NIJ communicates its research and evaluation findings through conferences and print and electronic media.

To find out more about the National Institute of Justice, please visit:

http://www.ojp.usdoj.gov/nij

or contact:

National Criminal Justice
 Reference Service
P.O. Box 6000
Rockville, MD 20849–6000
800–851–3420
http://www.ncjrs.gov